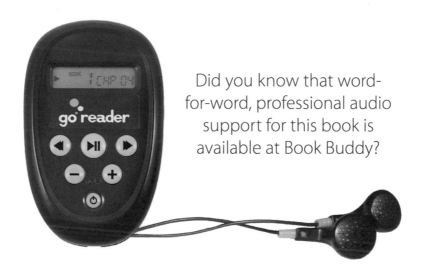

Did you know that word-for-word, professional audio support for this book is available at Book Buddy?

GoReader™ powered by Book Buddy is pre-loaded with word-for-word audio support to build strong readers and achieve Common Core standards.

The corresponding GoReader™ for this book can be found at: http://bookbuddyaudio.com

Or send an email to: info@bookbuddyaudio.com

AVAILABLE NOW
from Lerner Publishing Services!

The *On the Hardwood* series:

Atlanta Hawks	*Houston Rockets*	*Oklahoma City Thunder*
Boston Celtics	*Indiana Pacers*	*Orlando Magic*
Brooklyn Nets	*Los Angeles Clippers*	*Philadelphia 76ers*
Chicago Bulls	*Los Angeles Lakers*	*Phoenix Suns*
Charlotte Hornets	*Miami Heat*	*Portland Trail Blazers*
Cleveland Cavaliers	*Milwaukee Bucks*	*Sacramento Kings*
Dallas Mavericks	*Memphis Grizzlies*	*San Antonio Spurs*
Denver Nuggets	*Minnesota Timberwolves*	*Toronto Raptors*
Detroit Pistons	*New Orleans Pelicans*	*Utah Jazz*
Golden State Warriors	*New York Knicks*	*Washington Wizards*

To Order • www.lernerbooks.com • 800-328-4929 • fax 800-332-1132

ON THE HARDWOOD

ZACH WYNER

On the Hardwood: Sacramento Kings

MVP Books
2255 Calle Clara
La Jolla, CA 92037

MVP Books is an imprint of Book Buddy Digital Media, Inc., 42982 Osgood Road, Fremont, CA 94539

MVP Books publications may be purchased for educational, business, or sales promotional use.

Cover and layout design by Jana Ramsay
Copyedited by Susan Sylvia & Renae Reed
Photos by Getty Images

ISBN: 978-1-62920-180-1 (Library Binding)
ISBN: 978-1-62920-181-8 (Soft Cover)
ISBN: 978-1-62920-178-8 (eBook)

TABLE OF CONTENTS

On October 30, 2013, Kings fans packed Sleep Train Arena for the season opener against the Denver Nuggets, ready to celebrate. It was the first night of the 2013-14 season, a season in which Sacramento was expected to finish at the bottom of their division. But on this night, fans couldn't have cared less. All that mattered to them was that their beloved Kings were staying in Sacramento.

Before the game started, the man recognized as the savior of the franchise, computer software CEO Vivek Ranadivé, had a special message for the fans. Ranadivé, a slender man with gentle brown eyes, an easy smile, and wisps of grey in his

dark brown hair, strolled onto center court and took the microphone. Eager fans stood, a murmur filling the arena. "Sacramento," he said. "I have just one thing to say to all of you. And

New Kings' owner Vivek Ranadivé addresses the Sacramento faithful on opening night.

let's never forget that one thing. This is your team! And it's here to stay!" The joyful crowd roared, applauded, and rattled cowbells in approval.

That night DeMarcus Cousins scored 30 points, and the energized Kings beat Denver, 90-88.

DeMarcus Cousins' 30 points and 14 rebounds led the Kings to victory on Opening Night in 2013.

The Sacramento Kings traveled far and wide before landing in the capital of California. Since their arrival, they've grown into an institution—a team supported by fans every bit as anxious to win as its coaches and players. Kings fans have stood by their team through the best and worst of times. Throughout years of drought, when it seemed the Kings might never grow into a consistent winner, fans never gave up hope.

In the late 1990s, a combination of smart trades, great coaching, and excellent drafting rained good fortune on this team that always seemed to be building for the future. A strong crop of young talent sprang up in Sacramento and "The Greatest Show on Court" was born. For a few magical years, there was no better show in the NBA.

Sadly, the "Greatest Show on Court" dissolved before the Kings had a chance to lay claim to the franchise's second NBA crown. But the Sacramento faithful stood by their team. The Kings' success had proven that a team didn't need to be from one of the country's largest cities in order to be a contender. While some considered them underdogs, the Kings had the support of one of the greatest fan bases in the NBA. That support became especially important in 2013, when the Kings'

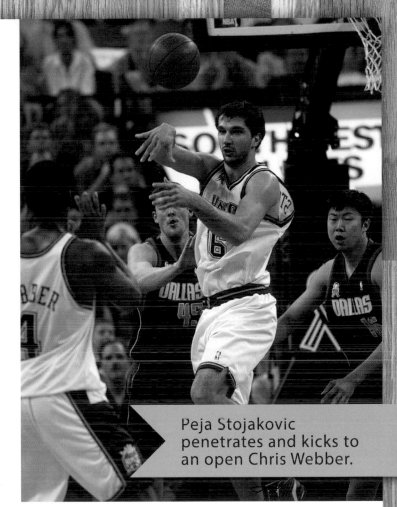

Peja Stojakovic penetrates and kicks to an open Chris Webber.

owners attempted to sell the team to a group that planned to move them to Seattle, Washington.

For some time it appeared that Sacramento, a city that provided one of the greatest home court advantages in the League, would join

Sacramento mayor and former NBA All-Star, Kevin Johnson, sits courtside with his wife on Opening Night.

Ranadivé already had some experience with underdog basketball teams.

A computer software engineer and businessman, Vivek Ranadivé had never touched a basketball in his life when he became the coach of his 12-year-old daughter's basketball team. But his lack of experience didn't bother him. Ranadivé observed his daughter's team play. Realizing that they didn't have many ball-handlers or shooters, he decided that his team would win with defense. He coached his girls to play a full-court press the entire game, every game. The strategy worked. The team went undefeated through the regular season and won a state championship.

Rochester, Cincinnati, Omaha, and Kansas City, as former hosts of this roaming franchise. But Sacramento mayor and former NBA All-Star Kevin Johnson rallied a group of investors headed by Vivek Ranadivé, and the NBA owners unanimously voted that Sacramento should be allowed to keep its Kings. As it turned out,

Ranadivé firmly believes that if a team works with what it has and develops creative solutions, it can overcome any obstacle. This kind of thinking will be welcome in Sacramento, as it has been quite a long time since the small-market Kings conquered the NBA's giants.

The last time the Kings stood at the top of the League was way back in 1951, the earliest years of the franchise, when they were known as the Rochester Royals. Back then the NBA—the product of the 1946 merger of the National Basketball League (NBL) and the Basketball Association of America (BAA)—was struggling to

stay afloat. In fact, before the 1950-51 season began, six of the NBA's 17 teams folded, leaving the League with only 11 teams. When another team

Rochester Royals guard Red Holzman drives around a defender during an NBA game circa 1950.

Bob Davies averaged 15 points and 5 assists for the NBA Champion Rochester Royals.

went under during the season, the Royals were one of just 10. However, while fewer teams meant less travel, it did not mean easier opponents. The best players of the failed franchises signed with the teams that were still standing, making the 10 surviving NBA teams that much stronger. Those 10 teams represented the cream of America's basketball crop—or at least, the best of the white players.

1951 was a complex time. The country suffered from deep racial divisions. Schools in the South were segregated, meaning that black and white children could not share classrooms. With many states going to extremes to prevent blacks from voting, change was not going to happen overnight. At this point in time, a number of courageous black athletes integrated into professional sports, propelling the country into a much-needed period of transformation.

By 1947, the great African-American boxer Joe Louis had been the heavyweight champion of the world for 10 years. That year, Jackie Robinson became the first black player to play Major League Baseball, and the Rochester Royals became the first NBL team to integrate, with the signing of William "Dolly" King. A former player for the New York Renaissance (also known as the Harlem Rens), William King played only one season with the Royals, but it was a meaningful one. He helped

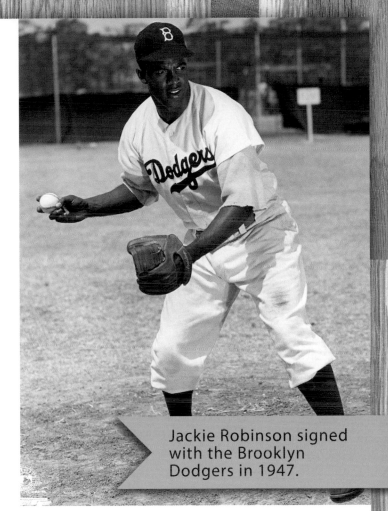

Jackie Robinson signed with the Brooklyn Dodgers in 1947.

the Royals win an NBL title. In refusing to be intimidated by racists, William King and black athletes like him were crucial parts of the Civil Rights Movement that changed America.

While the Rochester Royals did not have an integrated team in 1950,

The NBA Champion Rochester Royals team portrait.

they were leaders in other respects. Behind the play of Bob Davies, Bobby Wanzer, and Arnie Risen, the Royals beat the two-time defending champion Minneapolis Lakers and advanced to the NBA Finals to face the New York Knicks. Once there, the team took a commanding 3-0 series lead. Then, with Rochester on the verge of celebration, the New York Knicks stormed back, winning three straight and forcing the first Game 7 in NBA Finals history.

In Game 7, the stars came to play. Royals' Hall of Fame center Arnie Risen led both teams with 24 points and 13 rebounds, and the Royals opened up a 16-point first-half lead. That lead evaporated in the second half, as New York used a big third quarter to cut the lead to two. With 40 seconds remaining in the game, All-Star point guard Bob Davies broke a 75-75 tie by hitting two free throws. The Royals hung on to win 79-75 and earn their first and only NBA crown.

After advancing deep into the playoffs in 1953 and 1954, the Royals slipped a bit in 1955. The one positive result of this slide was the reintegration of the team with the drafting of power forward Maurice Stokes. Stokes made an immediate impact as a rookie, leading the team in points per game (16.8) and leading the NBA in rebounds per game (16.3). Together, he and fellow rookie Jack Twyman formed a high-scoring duo. While they were unable to lead the Royals back to the playoffs, Twyman and Stokes forged a lasting friendship that would inspire generations of fans.

Maurice Stokes won the Rookie of the Year award in 1956.

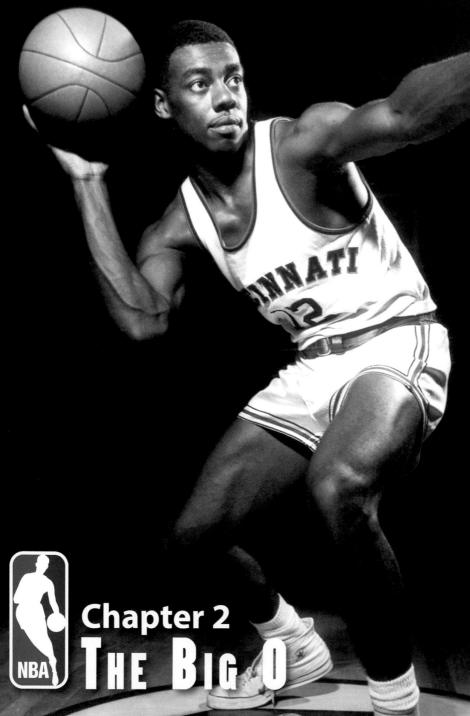

In 1957, the Royals moved to Cincinnati, Ohio. Although the team had been absent from the playoffs for two years, their time in Rochester had been extremely successful. During the team's 12-year stay, they featured nine Hall of Famers and won an NBA title. With young stars like Maurice Stokes and Jack Twyman, it seemed that the Royals were likely to resume their winning ways.

In their first season, the Cincinnati Royals were back in the playoff picture. Clyde Lovellette and Twyman led the team in scoring while Stokes had his best season as a pro, averaging 16.9 points, 18.1 rebounds and 6.4 assists. The Royals qualified for the playoffs. Then tragedy struck. During the last game of the season, Maurice Stokes hit his head on the court and was knocked unconscious. Although he was revived and continued to play in the game, his brain had been severely injured. Three days later, he played in his first postseason game in Detroit. On the flight back to Cincinnati, he suffered a seizure and went into a coma. By the time

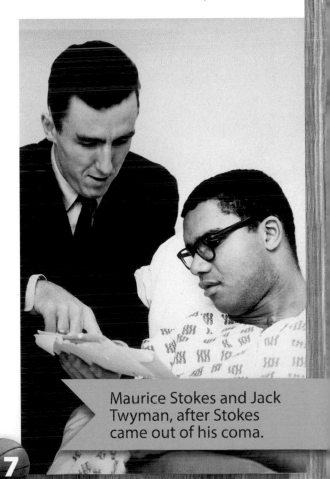

Maurice Stokes and Jack Twyman, after Stokes came out of his coma.

he regained consciousness, he was permanently paralyzed. Maurice Stokes would never play basketball again. That did not mean that Jack Twyman was about to stop being his teammate.

Maurice Stokes was in a terrible position. With his basketball career suddenly over, there was no way for him to pay his expensive medical bills. With Stokes facing financial ruin, Jack Twyman stepped up. Twyman brought his friend into his home, became his legal guardian and held fundraisers every year for the rest of Stokes' life in order to pay his medical bills. Because of Twyman's tireless efforts, Stokes survived for 12 years before passing away in 1970. In 2013, the NBA created the Twyman-Stokes Teammate of the Year award to honor the sacrifices Twyman made for his dear friend.

The loss of Maurice Stokes was a terrible blow to the Cincinnati Royals. The power forward was much

Twyman and Stokes enjoy a light moment during a physical therapy session.

more than a scorer. In fact, in 1958, he had become one of only two players (along with Wilt Chamberlain) to be in the top three in the League in rebounding and assists. Years after his death, Boston Celtics announcer Johnny Most compared Magic Johnson to Maurice Stokes because both men had great size and yet they could handle and pass the ball like smaller guards.

Luckily for the Royals, an equally well-rounded player was on his way to Cincinnati. He went by the nickname "The Big O."

In 1960, the Royals drafted University of Cincinnati All-American and Olympic gold medalist Oscar Robertson. In two seasons, Robertson took the team from 19 to 43 wins. He led the Royals in scoring and assists his rookie season and was named Rookie of the Year. In his second season, he accomplished something that no basketball player had done before and no player has done since.

A triple-double—when a player registers double-digits in three statistical categories such as scoring, rebounding and assists—is a rare achievement. Most NBA players never record one. Hall of Famers like Magic Johnson and Larry Bird registered between 11 and 17 in their best years. LeBron James has never gotten more than eight in a single season. None of these greats ever came close to what "The Big O" achieved in 1961-62, when he averaged a triple-double—30.8

Stiff Competition
Oscar Robertson finished third in the 1962 MVP voting behind Bill Russell and Wilt Chamberlain.

Oscar Robertson snags a rebound for the Cincinnati Bearcats.

points, 12.5 rebounds and 11.4 assists. Robertson's season stands as one of the greatest statistical achievements of all time, a true mark of greatness.

Oscar Robertson was born into poverty in Charlotte, Tennessee and grew up in a segregated housing project in Indianapolis, Indiana. Because his family could not afford a basketball, Oscar learned how to shoot by tossing tennis balls or rags bound with rubber bands into a peach basket behind his family's home. He attended Crispus Attucks High School in Indianapolis, an all-black school known for its outstanding teaching staff and famous alumni. In 1955, with Oscar Robertson dominating on the basketball court, Crispus Attucks became the first all-black school in the country to win a state championship. The next season, they became the first all-black team to win two in a row.

The Cincinnati Royals' two best seasons occurred early in Oscar's career. In the 1962-63 season, they made the Eastern Conference Finals against Bill Russell, Bob Cousy, and the mighty Boston Celtics. The Celtics had won four straight NBA titles, but Robertson, Twyman, and All-Star center Wayne Embry were intent on changing that. Momentum swung back and forth in the series, as the two teams battled through seven hard-fought games. Following an opening game upset win in Boston, Cincinnati took a 2-1 series lead with a 121-116 win

before an ecstatic home crowd. Nine Royals scored in double figures. Many wondered if Boston's remarkable run was about to end. Then Boston's offense erupted. Over the next two

Oscar Robertson launches a jump shot over the outstretched hand of 1963 NBA MVP Bill Russell.

Impressive Credentials

While in high school, Jerry Lucas was twice named Mr. Basketball USA. The only other players to accomplish this are Kareem Abdul-Jabbar and LeBron James.

games, the Celtics scored 253 points and won both contests.

Facing elimination, Robertson and Twyman battled back in Game 6, combining for 60 points and forcing a seventh and deciding game. But in Game 7, despite 43 points from "The Big O," the Royals came up short. The Celtics won 142-131 and went on to win their fifth straight title. Meanwhile, the Royals and their fans poured their hopes into the next season. Those hopes were kindled when the Royals signed another local

Hall of Fame point guard Bob Cousy shoots over Royals' reserve Adrian Smith at the Boston Garden.

legend—two-time Mr. Basketball USA, Jerry Lucas.

An Ohio legend who led Ohio State University to a national championship in 1960, Jerry Lucas was a 6'8" power forward/center who could score from inside and outside. In the 1963-64 season, that trend continued. Lucas and Robertson combined to average 49.1 points, 27.3 rebounds, and 13.6 assists. Robertson's 31.4 points and 11 assists per game earned him the NBA's Most Valuable Player award while Lucas averaged 17.7 points, 17.4 rebounds, and was named Rookie of the Year. With the addition of Lucas, the Royals won a franchise-record 55 games. However, entering the playoffs, their goal remained the same: Beat Boston.

After dispatching the Philadelphia 76ers in five games, the Royals entered their rematch with the Celtics feeling good about their chances. They had beaten Boston in seven of their 12 regular-season matchups. However, the NBA season had been a long, hard grind. By the time the 76ers were through with him, young Jerry Lucas was hobbled. Although he dressed for each game against Boston, his injuries prevented him from being the same player he had been during the regular season. Without consistent contributions from their young star, the Royals struggled to find themselves. Robertson and Twyman both played well, but Boston overpowered the Royals, winning the series in five games. It was a frustrating defeat for a team that felt they had the talent to win it all.

Chapter 3
MOVING ON OUT

Behind the stellar play of Oscar Robertson and Jerry Lucas, the Cincinnati Royals competed throughout the 1960s, making the playoffs six straight times between 1961 and 1967. In the 1965-66 season, Robertson and Lucas put up huge numbers. "The Big O" averaged 31.3 points, 11.1 assists, and 7.7 rebounds while Lucas averaged 21.5 points and 21.1 rebounds. But the East was a beast. Bill Russell's Boston Celtics and Wilt Chamberlain's Philadelphia 76ers were forces to be reckoned with. Beating both of them in a single postseason proved to be too great an obstacle for Cincinnati. By 1969, Jerry Lucas was gone. One season later, "The Big O" was sent to Milwaukee. In 10 remarkable seasons in Cincinnati, Robertson had averaged 29.3 points, 10.3 assists, and 8.5 rebounds, and cemented his legacy as one of basketball's all-time greats.

The Royals of the late 1960s were a reflection of their country. They were searching for an identity, trying

Jerry Lucas accepts the MVP trophy at the 1965 All-Star Game.

to figure out their place in the world. By 1972, the winning ways of the mid-1960s were but a memory, as was their time in Ohio. While their last season in Cincinnati had witnessed the arrival of Nate "Tiny" Archibald, the team finished out of the playoff picture for the fifth-straight year. The group of Kansas City businessmen that had bought the Royals in 1971 decided it was time to move. The team left Cincinnati and the Eastern Conference behind. They joined the Western Conference and split their time between Kansas City, Missouri and Omaha, Nebraska. Because Kansas City already had a baseball team named "Royals," the basketball team changed their name to the Kansas City/Omaha Kings.

In the Kings' first season in Kansas City/Omaha, Nate "Tiny" Archibald starred, putting up numbers as big as he was small. At 6'1", Tiny became the smallest player ever to lead the NBA in scoring. He also became the first player to lead the League in both points per game (34) and assists per game (11.4)—a feat that no NBA player has since matched. For his historic accomplishments, Tiny was named League MVP.

The Kings' most successful period in Kansas City came under 1979 Coach of the Year Cotton Fitzsimmons. From 1979 to 1981, the Kings made the playoffs for three straight years. Otis Birdsong, Scott Wedman, and University of North Carolina star Phil

Not-So-Tiny Numbers

Archibald's 34 points per game was an NBA record, and his 910 total assists broke the NBA single-season record.

Ford led a potent offensive attack, and the 1978-79 Kings went 48-34 and won their first division title since 1952. First-round playoff defeats in 1979 and 1980 spoiled the two best regular-season efforts the Kings had in Kansas City. However, with a win on the final day of the season, the 40-42 Kings snuck into the 1981 playoffs and shook up the basketball world.

The Kings' 1981 playoff run began with a 2-1 series victory over the Portland Trail Blazers. They pulled off the upset without starting point guard Phil Ford, who had been lost for the season to an injury in February. However, when they faced off with the No. 1-seeded Phoenix Suns, few

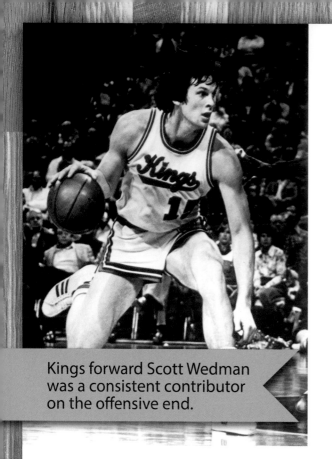

Kings forward Scott Wedman was a consistent contributor on the offensive end.

play the games.

Coach Fitzsimmons started 6'6" forward Ernie Grunfeld at point guard where he excelled, and reserve forward Reggie King caught fire. Together Reggie King, Scott Wedman, Ernie Grunfeld, and veteran center Sam Lacey played their best basketball of the season. They whipped Phoenix on the boards and extended the series to seven games. Sam Lacey joked, "We've got the slowest backcourt in the League, and the way we play we're probably killing CBS's ratings. But we don't quit." In Game 7, Ernie Grunfeld and Reggie King each stepped up with 23 points. The Kings won the series and advanced to the Western Conference Finals.

felt they had a chance. The Suns were an up-tempo team that ran like gazelles; the Kings were aging and slow. Then the Kings All-Star forward Otis Birdsong went down with an ankle injury in a lopsided Game 1 loss. Without their two starting guards, the Kings were thought to be finished. But as the saying goes, that's why they

Sadly, the Kings could not

continue their incredible run against Moses Malone's Houston Rockets. The next few seasons saw the departure of their best players, and by 1985, the franchise was in shambles. They packed their bags, moved west to Sacramento, California, and set up camp at the 10,000-seat ARCO Arena. In their inaugural season, the Kings sold out every single game.

After making the postseason in their first year in Sacramento, it took the Kings 10 years to make it back. During that stretch, fans cheered for the likes of Spud Webb, Brian Grant, Mahmoud Abdul-Rauf, and Olden Polynice. However, the player that outshined all others during this era was Mitch Richmond. From 1992 to 1998, Richmond led the Kings in scoring every season and was named

to six-straight All-Star teams. His 23.3 points per game are the fourth most in franchise history.

In 1998, Richmond's time in a Kings' uniform came to an end, when Sacramento traded him to Washington for the player who would become the cornerstone of the franchise.

From 1991 through 1998, Sacramento's offense ran through Mitch Richmond.

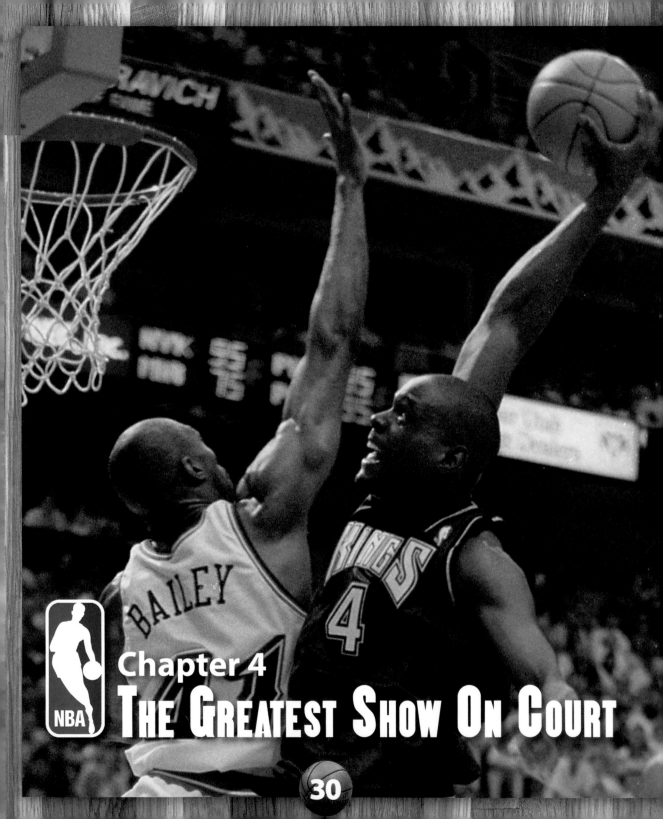

Chapter 4

THE GREATEST SHOW ON COURT

As a member of University of Michigan's "Fab Five," Chris Webber had achieved national stardom in 1991, when he and fellow Detroit natives Juwan Howard and Jalen Rose took the college basketball world by storm. Starting five freshman, the Michigan Wolverines made it all the way to the 1992 NCAA National Championship Game. After another strong showing in the 1993 NCAA Tournament, Webber entered the NBA Draft and was selected with the No. 1 overall pick.

During his first six NBA seasons, Webber performed at a high level, earning the Rookie of Year Award and making an All-Star Game. However, no one fully understood Chris Webber's potential until he joined coach Rick

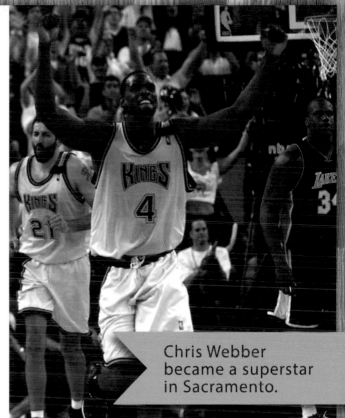

Chris Webber became a superstar in Sacramento.

Adelman in Sacramento.

In the strike-shortened season of 1998-99, Chris Webber's Kings finished with a record of 27-23 and made the playoffs. But the team's improved record didn't tell the whole story.

Board King
In his first season with the Sacramento Kings, Webber led the League with 13 rebounds per game.

The Big 5-0

The 2000-01 season marked the second time in franchise history that the Kings won more than 50 games. Robertson and Lucas led the team to 55 wins in 1964.

With flashy rookie Jason Williams in the backcourt, and outstanding passing big men Vlade Divac and Chris Webber in the frontcourt, the Kings were becoming more than just a winner; they were becoming a spectacle. Although they lost their first-round series to Karl Malone, John Stockton, and the powerful Utah Jazz in five games, the season ended with high hopes for the future.

Those high hopes were realized in 2000, when the Kings acquired veteran shooting guard Doug Christie and reserve point guard Bobby Jackson, and witnessed the emergence of Peja Stojakovic.

Suddenly, Sacramento was not just winning in front of the home crowd. They were winning tough road games, and they were doing it with a combination of ball movement and defense. After finishing the season with a franchise-record-tying 55 regular season wins, the Kings won their first playoff series in 20 years, defeating the Phoenix Suns three games to one. Although they were swept by the eventual-champion Los Angeles Lakers, the Kings had made their mark. Their starting five of Webber, Divac, Stojakovic, Williams, and Christie made the cover of Sports Illustrated, where they were labeled, "The Greatest Show on Court."

In a year marked by the tragic events of 9/11, the 2001-02 Sacramento Kings were a source of inspiration. Teammates Vlade Divac and Peja Stojakovic, natives of Serbia and Croatia, had seen their homelands fight a vicious war in the 1990s. Having once been a member of a country called Yugoslavia, Croatia had asserted its independence when the Soviet Union fell in 1991. What followed was a bloody struggle that turned former countrymen into bitter enemies.

Despite all that had taken place back home, Divac and Stojakovic shared an extremely close bond. In 2001, they organized a Basketball Without Borders camp that brought together teenagers and professional basketball players from the six republics of the former Yugoslavia. When asked about the camp, Divac said, "What we try to send to the kids is a message that they should believe in themselves and respect each other, have tolerance for each other and have fun." Divac's and Stojakovic's friendship was an echo of Maurice

Divac and Stojakovic share a laugh before the beginning of a game.

Stokes' and Jack Twyman's. They were teammates who saw past differences in race and nationality. They demonstrated what people are capable of when they let go of hatred and fear.

The 2001-02 Kings were more than a lesson in brotherhood; they were a lesson in teamwork. Like grandmasters of chess, they outsmarted and outplayed their opponents, and they ran away with a division title. They set a franchise record in wins (61), won the Pacific Division, and earned the No. 1 seed in the playoffs. With newly acquired guard Mike Bibby running the point, they shared the ball as well as any NBA team. Chris Webber and Peja Stojakovic spearheaded an offensive machine that featured seven players who averaged double digits in scoring.

In the first round of the 2002 playoffs, the Kings overcame a Game 2 loss at ARCO Arena to beat the aging Utah Jazz

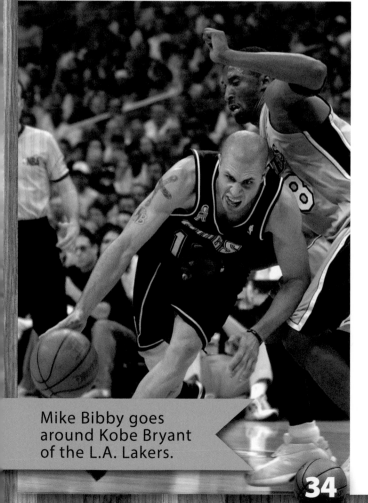

Mike Bibby goes around Kobe Bryant of the L.A. Lakers.

three games to one. In the second round, they faced another young, high-scoring opponent in the Dallas Mavericks. Dirk Nowitzki, Steve Nash, and Michael Finley formed a three-headed monster that many thought could give the Kings trouble.

After a Game 1 victory at ARCO, the Kings lost Game 2. Then, once again, the Kings demonstrated their maturity. With the series tied at one game apiece, Webber and Bibby went on scoring rampages. Sacramento won two straight games in Dallas, came home to ARCO and finished off the Mavericks in Game 5. The stage was set for an epic showdown. The two best teams all season long in the NBA—Sacramento and Los Angeles—squared off in the Western Conference Finals.

Chris Webber drives to the basket and shoots over Karl Malone of the Utah Jazz.

He's Number Ten

The University of Arizona retired Mike Bibby's No. 10 jersey. Bibby led the Wildcats to a National Championship in 1997.

The Kings huddle on the court during their Game 3 win in Los Angeles.

When Shaquille O' Neal, Kobe Bryant, and the two-time defending champion Los Angeles Lakers came into ARCO Arena and won Game 1 of the series, things looked bleak. Peja Stojakovic was sidelined by injury. Many doubted the Kings' ability to overcome the loss of home court advantage and their second leading scorer. But, after winning Game 2 at home, the Kings traveled to L.A. and beat the champions on their home floor. Second-year forward Hedo Turkoglu filled in nicely for Stojakovic, while Webber and Bibby shouldered the scoring load, and Doug Christie dominated on both offense and defense.

Following a close Game 4 defeat, the series returned to Sacramento.

Armed with cowbells, Kings fans cheered their lungs out as the game came down to the final minute. With Sacramento trailing by a point with 29 seconds remaining in the game, Vlade Divac blocked a shot by Kobe Bryant. Then, with eight seconds remaining, Webber passed to Bibby for a 22-foot jumper. Bibby sank it. The crowd went wild. The Kings had a 3-2 series lead.

Game 6 of the 2002 Western Conference Finals will live in infamy as long as there are Kings fans. With the score knotted at 75 entering the fourth quarter, the Kings had a chance to close out the series in L.A. and advance to their second NBA Finals. Then things got screwy. In the fourth quarter, Kobe Bryant didn't receive a foul, despite giving Mike Bibby a bloody nose. To add insult to injury,

Ready for the Second Season
The Kings won a franchise-record 10 postseason games during their memorable run in 2002.

the Lakers went to the free throw line 27 times to the Kings' nine. Los Angeles won 106-102. The frustration of the loss proved too much for the Kings to overcome. They lost Game 7 at home and their magnificent season came to a close.

The 2002 playoffs broke the hearts of the Sacramento Kings and their fans, but nothing could break the spirit of the franchise. This team that had moved so many times over the course of its history had developed a loyal following in Sacramento. Even when their winning ways began to fade, fans continued to embrace them, waiting patiently for the chance to cheer them to a championship.

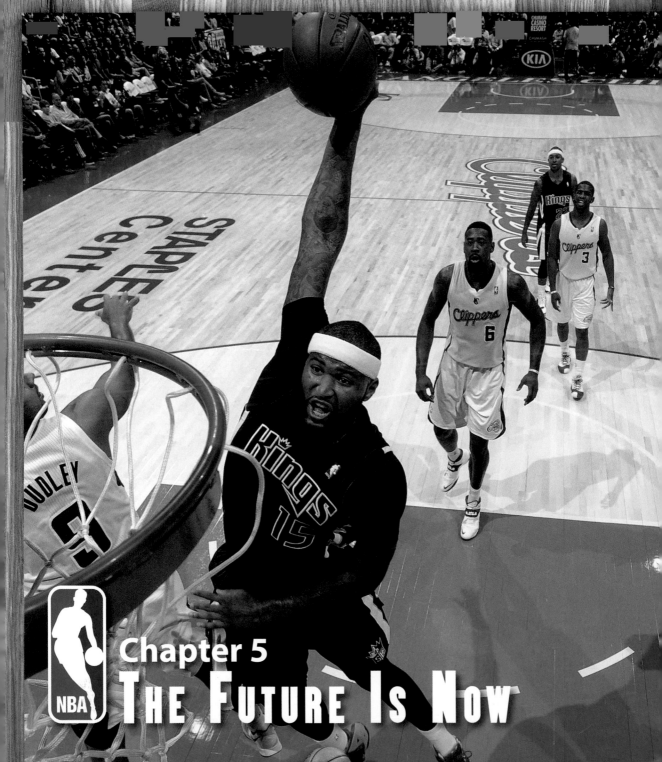

Chapter 5
THE FUTURE IS NOW

The Kings returned in 2003, ready to take what had been stolen from them—a trip to the NBA Finals. This would prove to be an especially challenging task, as the injury bug bit them early and often. Bibby, Stojakovic, Jackson, Turkoglu, and Scott Pollard all missed significant portions of the regular season with injuries. But the team demonstrated the will of a champion, winning 59 games despite the injuries. When playoff time came, they were as healthy as they had been all season, and confident that 2003 could be their year.

Sadly, the NBA crown would once again go to a Western Conference rival. After dispatching the Utah Jazz

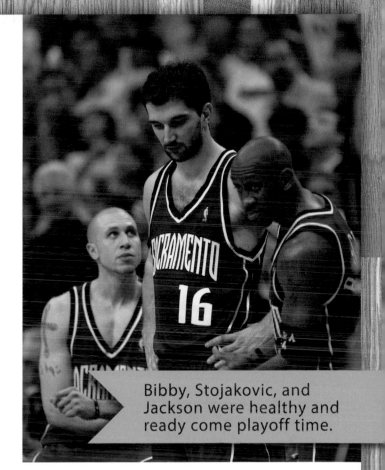

Bibby, Stojakovic, and Jackson were healthy and ready come playoff time.

in the first round, the Kings went to Dallas and won the opener, 124-113. Webber, Stojakovic, and the NBA's Sixth Man of the Year, Bobby Jackson, combined for 73 points. The Kings

Standout Sub
Fan-favorite Bobby Jackson averaged 15 points, four assists, and three rebounds during the 2002-03 season.

appeared destined for another trip to the Western Conference Finals. Then, in Game 2, Chris Webber went down with a devastating knee injury. Sacramento's best player was lost for the season. Although they fought valiantly in his absence, the Kings were unable to match Dallas' high-powered offense. They lost the series in seven games. Perhaps harder to stomach than the end of the season was the end of Webber's dominance. While the highly skilled big man was able to return halfway through the next season, he was not the same player.

The Kings' decline spanned the

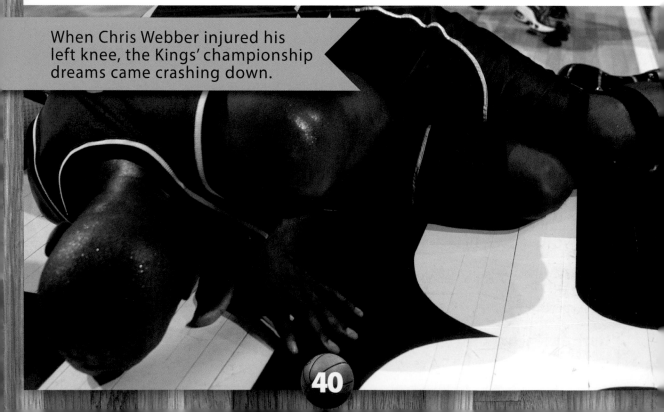

When Chris Webber injured his left knee, the Kings' championship dreams came crashing down.

next three seasons. By the midpoint of the 2004-05 season, Divac, Christie, and Webber were all gone, replaced by Brad Miller, Cuttino Mobley, and Corliss Williamson. Other changes included the trade of fan favorite Bobby Jackson for Bonzi Wells, the signing of free agent Shareef Abdur-Rahim, and the swap of Peja Stojakovic for Metta World Peace (then known as Ron Artest). The 2005-06 Kings weren't bad; they won 44 games and made the playoffs, but "The Greatest Show on Court" was merely a memory.

By the end of the 2006-07 season, Kings fans watched their team win just 33 games and finish outside of the playoff picture for the first time in eight years. Other

Bonzi Wells and Brad Miller provided the 2005-06 Kings with scoring and rebounding.

than the arrival of shooting guard Kevin Martin, who had grown into a premier scorer, there was little to cheer for. Frustratingly, missing the playoffs would again become a trend in Sacramento. Consistent play by Martin, World Peace, Brad Miller, and Beno Udrih was not enough to excite their fan base. After selling out every home game from 1999 to 2007, attendance numbers fell.

Maybe it was the departure of Mike Bibby—the last remnant of "The Greatest Show on Court"—that so disheartened their fans. Maybe it was that, after watching "greatness," Kings fans weren't so excited to shell out money for "good." However low Kings fans felt, nothing could have prepared them for 2008-09.

In a season in which the roster was drastically changed, the Kings won only 17 games. Despite having the League's worst record, they fell to fourth in the 2009 NBA Draft. They selected Tyreke Evans, a talented 6'6" guard out of the University of Memphis who made an immediate

Kevin Martin led the Kings in scoring for three consecutive seasons.

splash. In his first year with the Kings, Evans became just the fourth player in NBA history to average at least 20 points, five assists, and five rebounds in his rookie season, and was named Rookie of the Year. But following a string of disappointing seasons, the 2013 Kings, seven years removed from the playoffs, traded Evans to New Orleans. While it was hard for fans to part with a player of his caliber, their disappointment was diminished when Kevin Johnson and Vivek Ranadivé swooped in and saved the team.

The 2013-14 Sacramento Kings were a bit of a mystery. While there was no questioning the team's talent, many wondered whether they

Tyreke Evans makes an athletic move during the 2010 Rookie Challenge.

would ever be able to play with the chemistry required to compete with the best.

The man who many feel is the future of the Kings' franchise is

Wheeling and Dealing
The Kings sent Tyreke Evans to New Orleans for Greivis Vasquez and then sent Vasquez to Toronto for Rudy Gay.

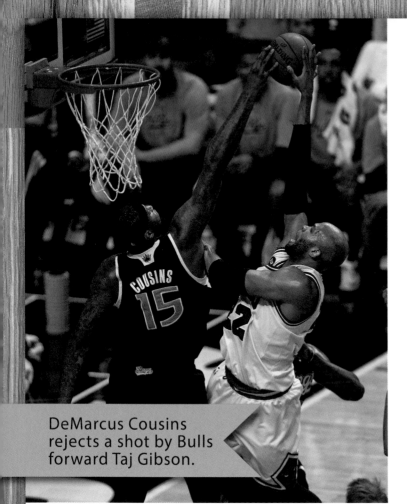

DeMarcus Cousins rejects a shot by Bulls forward Taj Gibson.

many years to come. In the 2013-14 season, the 23-year-old Cousins put up superstar numbers. By the season's midpoint, he was averaging career highs in points (22) and rebounds (12)—one of only five NBA players averaging more than 20 points and 10 rebounds per game.

A big man with big emotions, DeMarcus Cousins has a history of letting his temper get the best of him. However, his youth should not be forgotten. While he has been a pro since 2010, he is still young. Growing up is a process. Perhaps his increased scoring and rebounding are indicators of more than an improved game. 20-10

DeMarcus Cousins. At 6'11" and 270 pounds, Cousins has the size and skill to be a dominant big man for

Stand Out from the Crowd

In January of 2014, DeMarcus Cousins was named Western Conference Player of the Week, when he averaged 25 points and 13 rebounds and led the Kings to three straight wins.

players don't become that good by accident. Those numbers are a result of a tremendous work ethic, and a strong work ethic is a sign of maturity.

Playing alongside Cousins are two electric talents who have taken very different paths to Sacramento. 5'9" Isaiah Thomas starred at the University of Washington, but slipped to the 60th pick in the 2011 NBA Draft because of his lack of size. Meanwhile, NBA scouts drooled over 6'8", University of Connecticut forward Rudy Gay and made him a lottery pick in 2006. With his swift feet, incredible hops, and 7'3" wingspan, Gay was seen as a surefire scorer in the pros.

Since arriving in Sacramento, Thomas has used a combination of lightning speed, terrific handles, and excellent shooting to prove wrong all those who said he was too small to compete in the NBA. In three seasons, he has steadily increased his production. By the midpoint of the 2013-14 season, he was averaging

Isaiah Thomas surveys the floor, looking for an open teammate.

Rudy Gay brings the ball up the floor.

career highs in scoring (20.3) and assists (6.3).

Since his second year in the League, Rudy Gay has proven to be every bit the scorer that NBA scouts thought he would be, averaging 18 or more points per game every season. And yet, a Rudy Gay-led team has yet to win a playoff series. Many wonder whether Gay can be a premier scorer on a playoff contender.

Gay and Thomas provide the playmaking and outside shooting ability needed to complement Cousins' inside game. But more importantly, they are basketball players with something to prove. Thomas intends to prove that he can

In 2010, Bleacher Report named Gay one of the Ten Most Freakishly Athletic Players in the NBA.

be an elite point guard despite his small size. Now playing for his third NBA team, Gay desires to be known as more than a scorer; he wants to be known as a winner.

It's been quite a while since the Kings featured a team with three 20-point scorers. It may be that Thomas, Cousins or Gay will have to sacrifice some of those shots for the greater good. The Sacramento bench is loaded with talent. Young standouts Ben McLemore, Travis Outlaw, and Derrick Williams are hungry for the opportunity to show that they can excel in coach Michael Malone's system. Meanwhile, forwards Carl Landry and Reggie Evans have

At the 2014 Slam Dunk Contest, Ben McLemore demonstrates that there is no shortage of high-fliers in Sacramento.

demonstrated with previous teams that they can be difference-makers.

In 2013, Vivek Ranadivé's ownership group committed to keeping the Kings in Sacramento, saving the city's favorite franchise. The question that lingered on the minds of Kings fans was: What team did they save? Kings players have a long history of sacrificing for one another. Their fans hope that this young squad will continue that tradition. With this group of talented athletes, the time has come for Sacramento to be crowned Kings of the NBA.

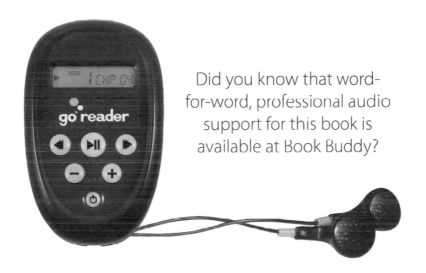

Did you know that word-for-word, professional audio support for this book is available at Book Buddy?

GoReader™ powered by Book Buddy is pre-loaded with word-for-word audio support to build strong readers and achieve Common Core standards.

The corresponding GoReader™ for this book can be found at: http://bookbuddyaudio.com

Or send an email to: info@bookbuddyaudio.com

8/16